THE THREE KINGS

In This World

Book 2

By

Allie Alberigo

The Three Kings – Book 2

Copyright © 2025 by Allie Alberigo

ii

All rights reserved. No part of this book may be used or reproduced in any form whatsoever without written permission except in the case of brief quotations in critical articles or reviews.

ISBN: 978-1-969978-04-3

Dedication

I have written many books and the dedication page is always one of the hardest parts to write.

To my beloved wife Nicole—I am so happy we found each other, and honestly, my life wasn't complete until I met you. Now because of you I feel like it is exactly where it should be. I am ready to spend the rest of my life with you. Your love and support are the foundation of everything I do. I love and thank you.

To my beautiful daughter—Kiara, the light of my life and the inspiration behind my every step. I hope you know that since you were born, the motivation behind everything I do is partly because of you. You have made me proud, made me smile, and you make me happy to be alive.

To my students, who challenge me daily to grow, learn, and pass on the wisdom of the martial arts. I am honored that you have, at one point, looked at me as your teacher. You keep me going on a day to day basis.

To my readers, who journey with me through my world of imagination and heart. You give me hope that, at my age now, I can continue to share my thoughts with you through books. So thank you for reading.

And to all of my friends, past and present, who have filled my life with laughter, strength, and unforgettable memories. I have only been close to a handful of people in my life. I want to thank you for being there every step of the way. This book is for you, from my heart.

Table of Contents

CHAPTER ONE

The Bully

The three boys watched as each second clicked away on the clock. The bell was just about to ring, signaling the end of their school day and the start of their weekend. Friday was a day that excited the boys. It was sparring night at the dojo, and the weekend was here.

"Okay everyone, gather your supplies and put them away. The bell is just about to ring," Mr. Spanno said in his raspy voice as everyone listened.

The bell rang, and in a mad rush, everyone grabbed their coats and hurried out the door. Merrick, Teal, and Cody joined the line of students leaving the classroom. They were lucky to be together in their final class of the day. Cody looked at the other two boys and said, "It's sparring night at the dojo. Can't wait."

The other two nodded with smiles on their faces as they walked into the hallway. Cody and Teal made fists and touched their knuckles together.

The hall was filled with excitement as hundreds of young students went to their lockers, gathering their jackets and preparing for the bus ride home. Merrick, Teal, and Cody continued toward their lockers as they turned to go down the steps of the two-story building. They reached the steps and started their descent when the hall of students suddenly parted.

A huge teenager in a black leather jacket pushed his way angrily through the crowd and stopped in front of another student. With all his might, he shoved the boy, who flew backward and slammed into a locker with a loud crash.

Someone in the crowd yelled out, "Fight! Fight!" Students came running. It seemed rather odd that people enjoyed watching two kids hurting each other for real. The three boys approached. Hank, the school bully in his black leather jacket, was picking on a much smaller Asian boy with glasses.

The boy was just getting up from being shoved against the locker when Mr. Spanno pushed his way through the crowd. "Let me through. Excuse me, please, move out of the way." He grabbed Hank by the jacket just before Hank could do more damage.

"Let's go, mister. You're coming with me," Mr. Spanno said as he dragged Hank down the hall.

Hank shook loose from Mr. Spanno's grip. "Get your hands off me."

Mr. Spanno looked at him in disbelief at how disrespectful he was for such a young man. He knew Hank was a troubled youth. "Looks like you're not going home after all. It's time for you to talk to the principal and spend some time in detention."

Hank smirked and even seemed to smile.

Cody walked over and reached down, offering his hand to the boy. "My name is Cody."

The boy ignored Cody's hand, picked up his books, and left without saying a word.

"Wow, that was kind of rude," Merrick said.

"Well, I'm sure he was embarrassed. Not really something to feel good about," Teal replied, clearing his throat.

"Yeah, I feel bad. I wish he would come down to the dojo. It would help him build his confidence and learn to protect himself from guys like Hank. We should invite him to Buddy Week next week, or Shihan or Renshi's Bully Proofing class."

Little did they know, this interaction was the start of a very strange friendship and exciting journey.

"Hey, there's Kiara," Cody said.

"Yeah."

Kiara came walking up, her pigtails bouncing as she moved.

"Hi, Senseis," Kiara said with a smile, nodding her head and bowing.

"Hello, Kiara-san," the boys replied in unison, nodding and bowing slightly back.

San is a word that shows respect in Japan.

All four walked toward their bikes in the bike rack outside, ready for the ride home. The boys looked after Kiara, after all, she was Shihan's daughter. Plus, she was a great kid, funny, and a strong martial artist. She also loved gadgets and spy stuff. Most people probably wouldn't know that because she dressed like a girly girl in fancy outfits and shoes.

The three boys and Kiara jumped on their bikes, and within a flash, they were on their way. They jumped curbs, zigzagged through trees, and pedaled as fast as they could. They rode as if they were racing in the local BMX competition held at the dirt bike park.

Kiara loved racing with the boys. She pedaled hard, and before long she was in the lead. Cody, Merrick, and Teal pushed harder to try to catch her. She looked back with a smile. "Shihan isn't gonna be mad at you if you beat me in a race."

The boys looked at each other and smiled, as if they were holding back because she was Shihan's daughter. But in reality, she was very fast and had great BMX skills.

They approached Castle Road and looked at each other before continuing on separately.

"See you at sparring class tonight, everyone."

They all acknowledged Kiara and continued in different directions toward their homes.

CHAPTER TWO

Sparring Class

Renshi walked up to the gong—a Japanese bell—which was hanging at the front of the dojo from the Kamidana shelf. He grabbed the stick with the large padded ball on the end and crashed it into the gong. The sound rang loudly throughout the dojo. The students ran to their line and sat in *Seiza*, the kneeling position with their legs folded under them, in a neat, straight line.

Renshi was Shihan's top student and was in charge when Shihan was not present. Renshi had been training since he was a teenager and was Shihan's right-hand man.

Shihan sat in *Seiza*, the traditional sitting position on his knees, facing the Kamidana. He joined his two hands together in a prayer position and began to recite the Ninja Poem.

"Chi heiya furu, kami no oshiewa, toko shi eni, tadashiki, kokoro, mio momoruran. Shikin Harimitsu Dai Komyo."

The class replied, "Shikin Harimitsu Dai Komyo." In unison, they clapped twice, bowed with their hands on the floor, sat up, clapped once more, then bowed again.

Shihan smoothly spun around to face the class as if he floated on air. This was a skill the ninja practiced called *Swari Waza*, and he sat up straight, awaiting the class leader's response.

Renshi called out, "Shisei O Tadashte, Shihan Ni Rei." The class bowed again, saying, "Onegaishimasu."

Onegaishimasu means "please teach me" in a respectful way. Renshi, Merrick, and the other black belts knew well what this meant, but Shihan explained it anyway to the rest of the class.

"Students, what I just spoke in Japanese is an ancient poem, taught to me by my Ninja teacher in Japan and taught to him by his teacher. For some of you, it is a way to focus your mind, your heart, and your body, to remember the masters who have come before you and pay respect to them now in the present. It is a way to say thanks, be humbled, and perfect your spirit. For other high-ranking students, you know exactly how much this means to you."

Renshi, Merrick, Teal, and Cody knew exactly what he was speaking of. This was a special incantation to help them harness their animal powers and ward off evil. Shihan winked at the boys. Kiara, fourth in line, winked back with a large smile. The boys didn't know if Shihan taught any of this to Kiara, but in any event, they all smiled and listened intently.

"It is time for sparring class. Remember, sparring is a skill developed through practice. Practice makes perfect, but only if you are practicing perfectly." This was one of Shihan's favorite sayings.

"We will work on our timing and the development of our reflexes. We shall practice moves we are excellent at, but mostly focus on things we are not so good at, so we become better at them."

The class said, "*Hai* (yes)," in unison and ran to get their padded fighting gear on. Shihan asked Renshi to take over and start the class. Within seconds, they were all geared up, paired, and sparring. Music played on the stereo, and there were nothing but smiles on everyone's faces. Shihan and Renshi coached and motivated each student, instructing them and giving pointers on how to improve.

Renshi and Shihan worked well together because they had been around each other almost every day for seventeen years. The class was filled with highly motivated, energetic people on a quest to be their very best.

Before the students knew it, Shihan rang the gong, and the class ran to line up. They finished the class the same way it had begun, except at the end of the claps and bows, Merrick called out, "Shisei o Tadaste, Shihan Ni Rei."

The class responded differently this time, "Arigato Gozaimasu (thank you very much)."

At this point, all the parents were gathering in the lobby to pick up their children. Soon it was just the three boys, Shihan, and Kiara. The boys would get a ride home from Shihan; after all, they had been training with him so long, he was like their martial arts father. Soon, everyone was home, and Shihan and Kiara were on their way to their house as well.

"Dad?" Kiara said.

"Yes, my love," Shihan responded.

"Today at school there was more trouble with that Hank boy. He was picking on some smaller kid, you know, the boy whose dad owns the Chinese medicine store you go to."

"Yes."

"Well, Hank pushed him really hard against the locker, but before he was able to hurt him, a teacher broke it up."

CHAPTER THREE

Dinner Conversation

Shihan made the turn down the street and slowly turned left into the driveway of their home. The house was at the end of a long driveway, high up the hill. Behind the house was a mountain, and to the left was a huge yard with a fire pit and a tennis court. When Shihan first saw the house, it was in the middle of a snowstorm and covered under two feet of snow. There was a family of six deer lying down in the snow. They saw Shihan and didn't even move. It seemed they trusted him and felt no fear.

Shihan put the car in park, turned off the ignition, and the car purred to a halt.

Kiara grabbed her backpack, and they made their way into the home. Kiara slid her backpack into the corner where they normally kept it and immediately looked into her turtle tank.

"Hey, Squirt, Scratch, and Gator, how are you guys today?" she asked in a motherly voice.

"Feed them while I start dinner for us. What do you want tonight?"

Kiara, all excited, turned and said, "Tostones and a veggie dog." This was one of her favorite quick meals.

Her dad reached for the frying pan and put it on the stove, then grabbed the olive oil from the kitchen cabinet.

"Kiara, how did that make you feel today when you saw that boy being picked on?"

"Well, Dad, to be honest, I was sad. People can be really mean sometimes, but I feel so bad he always gets in trouble."

"Kiara, are you talking about the boy who got picked on, or the boy who was doing the picking?"

"Oh, I feel bad that Christopher got picked on, but I also feel bad that the bully, Hank, feels like he has to be a bully. It almost seemed like he was happy that he was in detention, almost like he did it just to be there."

"Well, kiddo, sometimes kids who are bullies do it because they are treated that way at home, or they have other issues and don't know how to deal with them. There is a saying: hurt people hurt people. Also, it is important to remember that sometimes kids just want to feel popular and get attention. Even though this is the wrong way to do it, they are reaching out for help."

"Exactly," Kiara said. "I know that deep down inside, Hank is probably a good person, but he just needs to find that strength inside him, just like we teach the kids at the Stranger Danger; the Bully Proofing seminar at the dojo."

"Kiddo, I love you," Shihan said, looking at his daughter with such affection. "You are so smart. One day, you are going to be the President of the United States, or the next star of *American Idol.*"

Shihan held the spatula in one hand and started singing a song Kiara had never heard. She laughed and smiled.

"Now go run and wash your hands. Dinner will be ready in a few minutes. At dinner, I want to tell you a story about a boy I met when I was in high school."

CHAPTER FOUR

The Story

Shihan and Kiara sat at their dinner table and began to eat.

"Em…that is good stuff," Kiara said. She loved her Tostones, fried plantains from the banana family. They weren't sweet but crunchy, like French fries. Kiara had been a vegetarian her entire life, and Shihan had been a vegan for over fifteen years.

"So, Dad, tell me that story," she said. She loved her dad's stories.

"Well, there was a young man in about tenth grade. He had long hair and played in a rock band throughout his life as the guitar player and lead singer. Because he was different, and had long hair, some kids used to try to pick on him. For no reason at all, they didn't like him.

He spent most of his time avoiding them and taking alternate routes to his classes."

"Was that boy you, Dad?"

"Shhhh. Don't interrupt me while I have my story flowing," he said, smiling.

"Anyway, there was a small Chinese boy who was what they called a nerd. He was smart and always had a stack of books in his hands. Most of the time, the football team would pick on him, knock his books out of his hands, push him, and call him names."

"Wow, that stinks," Kiara said with her mouth full of food.

"Well, one day, the boy who spent most of his time avoiding these bullies, always defended by the other boy, was watching as the football players picked on him. He was in a fight with the same football team, and it was four to one. The young Chinese boy ran into the middle of the group and defended him, using martial arts skills. It was like one of those karate movies."

"I know it was you, Dad."

"Well, this time, when it happened, there were too many for me to handle."

"I told you it was you," she said, pointing excitedly.

"What I meant to say was that the boy, meaning me, was outnumbered and in trouble, and out of nowhere comes this nerdy little boy doing flips, cartwheels, and jump kicks. Before you know it, all of the bullies were running away."

The older boy was in shock and turned to the littler boy. "Why did you let me stick up for you this entire year when you were better than me at martial arts? I didn't know you knew martial arts."

The smaller boy reached out his hand and said, "My name is Christopher, and…"

"No way, don't tell me," Kiara interrupted. "Is that Christopher's dad from Christopher's Herb Shop?"

"Yes, kiddo, the one and only. The entire time, I thought this little boy was unable to defend himself, but you see, his dad had told him to never fight unless his life depended on it."

"Well, being picked on is a time to defend yourself, right, Dad?"

"It really all depends. Christopher never felt like he had to; I guess he didn't feel threatened enough."

"Then why did he help you?"

"I asked him the very same question. You know what he told me?"

"No, what?"

"He told me that he wasn't threatened himself all those times and knew he would be okay, but he felt that I was in danger and had to jump in for a friend."

"Wow, this all makes sense now. Is that why Christopher's dad never charges you for herbs?"

"Exactly," Shihan smiled, using Kiara's favorite word.

Shihan finished his last bite on his plate.

"Finish up, kiddo, and go take that shower."

"Okay, Dad, that was an awesome story."

"It's true, every word of it," Shihan replied.

CHAPTER FIVE

On Their Way

Saturday morning came in a flash, and Cody, Merrick, and Teal were up early, as they had been doing for years. Already en route, they had one last stop before their final favorite destination. Riding as if they were in a BMX race, they soon came to a skidding halt in front of Shihan's house.

Kiara, waiting at the window, yelled, "Bye, Dad! I'm going with the guys to train." She came running outside and, in a single leap, jumped off her step and rolled, a classic ninja move. Without a break in her stride, she grabbed her bike leaning against the house and was off pedaling. Immediately, the boys were trying to catch up with her.

"Slow down Kiara! It's not a race," Teal yelled out.

"Yeah, we don't want to be exhausted by the time we get there. Master Macgregor promised to teach us some martial arts today," Cody said, taking a breath.

"Okay, okay, as long as you admit you are all slow pokes," she smiled.

The boys caught up, and soon they were riding together. They made a right turn to take their shortcut through the park when they saw a boy on his front lawn raking leaves. They immediately noticed an older man holding his hand up as if he were going to hit the boy. The boy was Hank, the bully from school.

"Wow, I guess he finally gets what he deserves," said Merrick.

"That's not nice. Maybe he's the way he is because of the way he is treated all the time."

"Kiara, don't," Teal warned.

Kiara immediately turned toward Hank's house and rode up to the curb. "Hey, Hank!" she yelled.

The older man lowered his hand.

"Go away, Kiara! Get lost!" Hank barked. The man smacked Hank on the back of the head.

"Yeah, get lost, little girl!" The old man shouted.

Kiara put her foot on her pedal and pushed down hard; her back tire spun as she left. "Bye, Hank! We'll see you in school."

When the man looked over, his eyes seemed to flash red, then returned to normal. Kiara looked at him and quickly turned away.

Once she caught back up to the boys, she said, "Did you guys see that? Did you see his eyes?"

"I did. That was very weird, something isn't right there," Merrick said.

"I didn't see anything," said Cody.

"Me neither."

"Well, I did, and I'm going to ask Master Macgregor about it," Kiara replied as they made it through the park and entered the woods. Kiara was first; she hit a dirt mound, and her bike flew through the air. She released one hand from the handlebars and tilted her bike to the side as she performed her motocross trick. The boys did their own tricks.

They continued on for miles, racing in and out of trees, ducking under low-lying branches, and jumping over rocks and hills. Their final destination was the goal, but they enjoyed every step of the way getting there. This was a great day for them.

CHAPTER SIX

Master MacGregor's House

The boys passed through a clearing in the woods when, all of a sudden, Master MacGregor's house came into sight, a familiar place with a huge history. Cody, Merrick, and Teal had spent a great deal of time with Master MacGregor since their last adventure, honing their skills as Sennin—wizards.

Just recently, Shihan Allie had started sending his daughter Kiara to train with the boys, but she knew nothing of the "Three Kings." The boys would take time away from Kiara, practicing their magic as well as discussing some of the secrets, but Master MacGregor, the Sennin, would teach Kiara just as Shihan taught the boys: through stories and secret poems. The goal, of course, was to develop a habit so that Kiara would know what to do without really knowing she actually knew it. All he had to do was tell her the secret, and soon she would be able to put the clues together and perform as a wizard. Plus, Kiara was a bright girl, and she knew there was more to the training than they led her to believe.

"Kiara-san," Sennin spoke in a soft voice, "it is time for you to work on your daily meditation and your chant and poem. I want you to go to the waterfall on the north side of the property, sit in Anza, the cross-legged position, and start your practice. I have to work with the boys for a while."

"Hai (yes), Sennin," she replied, and within a flash she was off running.

"Boys, *Watashi no tokoro ni kite kudasai* (please come here)."

The boys ran up without a second of hesitation; they knew it was rather impolite to make their sensei wait. The boys stood at attention in front of their instructor.

"Hai, Sensei (yes), sir." Cody, first in line, spoke loud and clearly.

"*Shisei o tadaste, Sennin ni Rei,*" Sennin continued, which means, "present yourself to your sensei and bow."

They followed the command and bowed, saying "*Onegaishimasu,*" a formal way to ask the teacher, "Please teach me." Sennin bowed back with a smile. He loved his students as if they were his own children, just like most martial art instructors do.

"Boys, it has come to my attention that there has been a breach. Someone has managed to make it back to our realm from the past, and they intend to take over the world and wreak havoc."

The boys tried not to look at each other as their mouths dropped open.

"I know this sounds scary, and it is, but this is something only we can handle, and we can't tell anyone."

"Why don't we just tell the police or maybe the military? Why don't we call in the Navy SEALs?" Merrick replied. "Shihan always says they are one of the most elite fighting forces in the world."

"Boys, what we believe in our world is one thing, but you have seen things in another world on your last adventure. People do not believe that magic really exists. That is something only you can change if you believe. Others will just pretend nothing is going on, and that is where the danger lies."

Merrick spoke in a scratchy voice, like he had a frog caught in his throat. "Why can't we just tell the SEALs? I'm sure they would believe us."

"The answer is simple. The evil that exists is very good at turning good people into bad ones. If it gets them to turn, then we will not be able to do anything. We may be locked up forever and be so outnumbered that there is no going back. We need to keep this between us."

"Who is the evil?" Cody asked.

"This I do not know. It can come in many forms. Most likely, it may have inhabited a living form and taken over their body, or even a few people's bodies. I am sure it will do its best to change many people and start to build its army. One thing I can tell you is that it is close, and it is trying to find the book."

"I thought we were able to leave the land of the Three Kings and hide the book away forever, keeping that land locked up," Merrick said.

"Well, I did as well, but something must have gone wrong," Sennin replied.

"It is time for your training. Let's not talk of bad things anymore. You will need to be at your most powerful when needed. Kiara must be trained as well, and I think it is time we speak to her and let her know of her powers."

"That should be fun! Can we at least play with her a little?" Teal asked with a smile on his face.

"Well, that is something you may want to ask Shihan about," Sennin replied with a look on his face.

"Never mind. Forget that I mentioned anything. It doesn't sound like a good idea if I have to ask permission," replied Teal.

"Kiara is at the waterfall on the north side of the property. Go to her and bring her back here in twenty minutes; we will have tea and talk."

CHAPTER SEVEN

Kiara's Training

Before you could see, the boys were off and running. This time they did it like ninjas, jumping over fallen trees, dive-rolling over branches, and cartwheeling and flipping every chance they could get. When they approached, they stopped running and went into stealth mode, walking as silently as a cat. This special walk was called Shinobi Aruki; the ninja stealth walking.

You could hear the sound of the waterfall pounding down on the lake. As they peeked their heads around the large oak tree, they could see Kiara sitting in Anza, meditating and chanting. She let out a sound that seemed to vibrate in the boys' stomachs. The sound was "Om." This sound was taught to them by Shihan at the dojo. He explained it as the sound that vibrates through everyone. It is the sound that created the universe. It is a universal energy.

As Merrick, Teal, and Cody got closer, they saw Kiara in such a peaceful state, with a huge smile on her face. Meditation cleansed the soul and relaxed the mind and body. She had been doing it since she was a baby.

"Whoa, what is going on? What is that?" Teal said in a rather squeaky voice as he pointed toward the waterfall. The boys noticed that directly in front of the waterfall, rocks were floating in the air. Many little creatures gathered around Kiara, like squirrels, chipmunks, birds, and even a white wolf, an eagle, and a bear, all sitting in meditation and chanting the same sound.

The boys stepped out of the clearing. Teal stepped on a branch lying on the ground, and it cracked. Kiara turned and slowly opened her eyes, breaking her concentration. All the rocks crashed back into the lake. The animals slowly walked away, and without Kiara noticing, the forest was empty again.

"Kiara, how did you learn that?" Merrick asked.

"Do what? How to meditate? Oh, my dad taught me since I was a baby."

"Well, not so much the meditation, but the other stuff," Cody said, looking shocked.

"What other stuff?"

"The floating rocks and the animal thing."

"How did you know what I was thinking? How did you get into my imagination? Is that some sort of trick?"

"Not imagination, Kiara. That was real. The rocks were really floating, and all the animals were gathered around in meditation with you. It was real," Teal said in a whisper.

"Yeah, right! Stop messing with me. I know I am the youngest one here, but that's not nice."

"Kiara, this is real. Trust us. We really wanted to joke with you, but we thought Shihan would be upset. We love you and your dad, and would never do that to you. Seriously," Teal said.

Kiara, still in disbelief, said, "Well then, how did I do it? Show me."

"We don't have to show you. You already know how. This time just do it with your eyes open. Watch, we will sit with you."

The boys sat next to her on the rock and crossed their legs. They put their hands on their knees and joined the thumb and middle finger together. Kiara did the same. She closed her eyes and began chanting "Om."

"No, Kiara, do it with your eyes open," Merrick said softly. Kiara opened her eyes and began the chant. The boys joined in. Within minutes, the rocks started to rise out of the water and float, and the animals appeared one at a time on the hill. The sound of powerful wings came to a halt as a beautiful eagle perched on a rock, and beside it came a bear and a white wolf.

Kiara started to smile, though she was still in disbelief. The animals chanted, and she continued. A small tear formed in her eye as she realized all her imagination was real. She had always wanted this to happen, but most of the time she thought of it as just a dream. Now her dreams had become a reality.

After about ten minutes, Merrick interrupted her. "Kiara, Kiara." He nudged her. She was smiling from ear to ear. Once again, the rocks crashed back into the lake, and the animals walked away. This time, the wolf and bear stood on their hind legs, did a single-legged bow with one paw down, and nodded their heads. They then returned to all fours, walked slowly away, and disappeared from sight.

"Kiara, Sennin wants us to meet at the house, so let's go. He has much to explain to you," Cody said.

"Ah, ah, okay, let's go," Kiara said in an unsure voice, still trying to soak in what had just happened.

"Let's do it," Teal said, taking off in a flash.

"The last one to the house is the king of the slowpokes, hotoni Osoi Ranna!" Kiara was off running.

"Not again, she always has to be first," Teal muttered. They were off and running.

CHAPTER EIGHT

The First Magic Lesson

All four young people sat waiting on the bridge out front of Sennin's house. Off to the side was a small set of Tatami mats, the traditional Japanese mat used in martial arts schools in Japan and dojo's around the world. On top of that was a small table with a beautiful teapot, steam visibly pouring out of it. There were six small teacups, beautifully decorated.

Sennin's Soji Screen front door slid open, and he came walking out. He was in full uniform, the karate gi. He walked to the table and motioned for everyone to come and sit with a simple wave of his hand as he bowed. The four walked up, took off their shoes, and sat with their legs crossed under the table.

Kiara looked over at the empty seat and teacup and asked, "Sennin, who is that for?"

Before she could finish her sentence, the door slid open again. A huge smile came across Kiara's face. It was Shihan, her dad. The boys immediately stood up with Kiara, and they bowed. Shihan approached, slid off his shoes, and sat in anza a cross legged position at the table.

Sennin spoke first. "Kiara, this is something you may not understand at first, but it is real. You have been training for this day since you were twenty months old, joining your dad in classes at the dojo. You have been training to be a ninja, but most of all, you are in a **select** group of individuals called

'The Kings.' You are of royalty, and your family line stems back to the early Shogun of Japan. But not just Shogun. A special breed of people that have been keeping a balance in the universe of happiness, health, and safety for thousands of years-the Ninja. There are many people who would love to corrupt or upset the balance and bend it for their own selfish reasons, but we are the chosen ones, and we have to keep the world safe."

"Dad, oops, I mean Shihan, why don't we do like you say and call in the Navy S.E.A.Ls, the Rangers, the C.I.A., or other countries' special forces military?"

"Yeah, that is what I asked," replied Merrick.

"It is not that easy. These special forces groups are amazingly trained individuals and masters of what they do, but what they do is related to this physical world. What we are talking about is not. The force we are talking about can only be controlled by special individuals, such as the Kings. For some reason, we have been blessed to take on this job, and for generations, we have protected its secret as well as its powers from the evil that lurks every day."

"As Sennin told the boys prior, somehow this evil has come from another dimension and entered our world. We are in charge of finding out what it is, as well as training for the day when it shows itself to us."

"But what is this evil? Why didn't I know about it?" Kiara asked.

"Kiara, I know you are my daughter, and it seems that I have been keeping this from you, but it is not a secret. It is something that you are only now old enough to understand. You have had these special powers since you were a baby, and before your mom passed away, she and I wondered why things would float over your crib and your bottle would appear on the nightstand. We thought we were going crazy, but in reality, we knew it was you and your powers all along. You see, my love, you have the power to communicate with all animals and plants and to move things with your mind."

"Cool," Kiara said, smiling as she elbowed Merrick. "You are never, ever going to win a race again." She laughed.

Sennin chimed in, "We are not sure what we are up against, and we do not know who we are dealing with. I only hope that they have not been here much longer than we think. We hope this power will have had only a small amount of time to build its army."

"What do we do? How do we find out? What?" Cody asked, but Shihan quickly cut him off.

"Do not do anything other than keeping your eyes open. Do not try to change anything. Go to school, train, and keep enjoying your life. The natural order will alert us and give us certain clues."

"This day, I am sure, is not what you expected, but the day is the lesson. Keep training and we will see you Saturday," Sennin said in a pleasant voice.

Shihan took his last sip of tea, placed the cup down on the table, and both he and Sennin walked back into the house.

"Kiara, I will see you at home. Oh, and boys, keep an eye on her. I am afraid now that she knows her powers; she will be getting into some mischief."

The three boys bowed and replied, "Hai Shihan, arigato gozaimasu (Yes, thank you very much)."

Soon they were up and walking back toward their bikes.

"Hey guys, do you mind if I take a few minutes and sit and soak this all in? I want to go back to the waterfall." Kiara spoke.

The three boys looked at each other and shrugged. "I guess, but you heard what your dad said, no mischief," Merrick said, spoken like a big brother.

"I promise, I just want to think a bit," Kiara said. She had other plans, but it did not involve mischief.

"Why don't we just stay in the field and practice our weapons with our chants? Now that Kiara knows everything, it is free game."

"Kiara, this is for you," Teal said. He reached into a bag and pulled out his favorite weapon, the Kusari Gama, the sickle Kama and chain. Kiara loved practicing with this weapon, even though it was Teal's specialty.

"Here, take it with you. Be careful, it is a dangerous tool!"

CHAPTER NINE

Meeting Her Spirit Power

Kiara took a good grip of her Kusari Gama and hung the long chain and hoop over her shoulder. She walked off into the woods along the path. She ended up at a small shrine that Sennin had built and would often take the four kids to for meditation. In fact, this was the place where Kiara first imagined things happening, like animals gathering and things floating. This place was also very special to her because whenever she missed her mom, she would think about her and the fun times they had. Kiara's mom had passed away when she was about four years old.

Kiara kneeled in front of the Torii gate in seiza and bowed. She closed her eyes and sat quietly, placing both of her hands together in a prayer position. She clapped twice and bowed, then clapped again, bowing one final time just like they would do at the dojo before and after a class.

She then sat quietly. A small tear ran down the side of her face when a faint white shadow appeared in front of her. Kiara opened her eyes, and a smile came to her face.

"Mom?"

The figure was indeed her mom. She was an angel and stood there right in front of her. Kiara could see through her, but she was there.

"Mom, is that really you? What is this all about? What is going on? What are you doing here? I thought you were…"

"Kiara, I have come to you many times in your meditation and in your dreams, and I have told you before, you will never be alone. I am still in your life, just not in the way most people know. I will never leave you, and I am here to protect you and give you advice just like I did when you were a baby."

"But Mom, why did you have to go?" The tears became thicker.

"I didn't go by choice, my little girl. I left because my body was sick, but my spirit and my energy will be around forever. Remember one thing: life is precious, and it is something that we should never take for granted. So live each day as if it were a special gift. Just like Daddy always tells you, there are no guarantees in life. Time is just a quick passing thing."

"Mom, what about these new powers, or from what dad tells me, powers I had all along, but didn't know about."

"Well, my baby, you are a very powerful young lady, I knew this from the minute you were born. When I looked into your eyes, I saw something so special. Even people, and other children were drawn to you. People just wanted to be around you."

Kiara started to cry again.

"Don't cry, my little girl. I will be with you always, and remember, I love you more than you can ever imagine. Your dad worships the ground you walk on. You, my little girl, are destined to do incredible things. This is not the last time you will see me. If you ever need me, just call out my name. I promise to be there, and now that you realize your powers, I am even closer to you then ever before."

Her mom started to fade away.

"Mom, Mom, don't go!" Kiara cried.

Her mom faded out, then her voice spoke softly, "Don't worry, Kiara. I am not gone. As I said, call on me and I am there."

"Mom, are you my protector spirit?"

"Yes, my child, I am."

Kiara sat for a few more minutes, bowed again as she did when she arrived, and stood, wiping the tears from her eyes. Within minutes, all four Kings were on their way back home.

CHAPTER TEN

The Question

"D addy," Kiara spoke softly at the dinner table.

"Yes, my love."

"Why is it we never speak of Mommy?"

"Well, kiddo, it's not that we never speak of her. It's just a very uncomfortable situation for me to talk about. Why do you ask this now?"

"Today when I was meditating at the shrine, I saw her."

"You saw your mom? How so?"

"Well, she came to me and spoke to me while I was sitting at the Torii gate. She told me that she was my protector spirit."

"I knew that already. She is mine as well. Every time I need something or I am feeling down, I can just talk to her. She listens, and sometimes in my meditation, she talks back as well."

"How did Mom go away?"

"When you were born, Mommy had some complications, and the day you turned four, she got very ill and the doctors couldn't save her."

"Daddy, is that a tear? Are you crying?"

Shihan rubbed his eyes as if there was something in one of them. "Kiara, you have seen me cry many times before. You know I am a crybaby when I watch movies or television, and even when you do things that make me happy, like when you rode your bike for the first time. I am not afraid to cry. When I think of your mom, I miss her dearly, as you do, I am sure."

"Yes, sometimes I wish she was here with us at dinner, going to the dojo, or even to the movies. But like you said, she is with us everywhere. I just wish my friends could meet her and see why I loved her so much."

"I do too. Do you see why it is hard to talk about? But I am glad that we got it out and broke that barrier. Sometimes children lose their parents and never talk about it. They hold those feelings deep inside, and it leaves a huge hole in their hearts. We both know it is sad that Mom is not here with us physically, but we also know that in life there are no guarantees. Life is sometimes short for some. But we must remember the good things, the good times, and always realize that those people are not gone in spirit. They only go away if you let them. Please always remember that."

"I will. But now I can talk to Mom anytime. I can even see her."

"That is amazing, kiddo. I am so happy that you are able to do this finally, but I think you could always do that."

CHAPTER ELEVEN

The Army of Evil

The sounds of Kia, the spirit shout of a karate person, echoed loudly in the dojo. Many young teenagers were lined up in a horse stance, delivering punches as the instructor gave commands loudly.

"Ichi, Nee, San, Shi," he counted in Japanese as the class followed each move.

"I am your instructor. I am not a babysitter. You come here to learn how to be fighters, and you do not come here so I can treat you like little babies. Do you understand me?"

"Ous," they replied, with the typical karate style answer.

"We are preparing for something much bigger than you ever imagined, and soon it will be time for you to help me with my mission. Are you ready to follow me, or are you going to wimp out?"

"We will follow!" the class yelled all together.

"Good. Start your kumite drills. Start fighting."

A young man ran up and said, "Should we go get our gear on?"

"I asked you before, are you wimps or not?"

"We are not wimps!" the class yelled out as one.

"Then get out there and fight. So what if you get a broken nose or a bloody lip? This is the real deal, and you must learn how to fight."

The class started fighting each other. But it was not the same as a normal martial arts class. This was like a pack of wild animals, just beating each other up. It was a frenzy, like when sharks attack in the ocean.

The Sensei sat back and smiled. He giggled under his breath. It was the early stage. He walked over to the phone on the wall, slowly picked it up, and dialed. The phone rang once, and on the other line, a deep voice answered, "Yes?"

"The training is underway. I have planted the seeds, and I think I have a good group of young warriors, Master. We are on our way."

"Great. This is only the beginning."

The man's face came into view, and his eyes glowed red as he turned and hung up the phone. On the other end, the phone went to a quiet dial tone. The Sensei hung up his end and watched as the young students beat each other up. They seemed to really enjoy the blood, the pain, and the nastiness of the activity. He had an evil smile on his face the whole time.

CHAPTER TWELVE

The Clue

It was Monday, and the four kids were back at school, placing their bikes on the racks and locking them up. They saw Hank getting out of a car, and as he did, they Kiara noticed he had a black eye.

"Hey guys, do you see Hank has a black eye? I bet his dad hit him after we left this past weekend."

"Yeah, I don't doubt it. His dad seemed like a really mean person," Teal replied. Cody and Merrick just shook their heads.

Kiara started to walk toward him, but Merrick lightly grabbed her arm.

"Don't, Kiara. This is none of our business. We have more to worry about than this."

"No. If we don't help here, we are not doing the world any good, now are we? Plus, Master MacGregor and my dad, Shihan, said to go about living our lives like normal. To me, this is normal."

Kiara Ignoring the comments, took off in a slow jog and ended up right next to Hank.

Hank looked over at Kiara.

"What's up?" Kiara asked.

Hank looked away. "Nothing," he said, trying to hide his eye.

"Hey, what happened with your eye?" Kiara spoke softly.

"Nothing. I walked into a door."

"Well, that is one strong door." She giggled. Hank smiled at her.

"Hey Hank, if you ever want to talk, me and my friends are here for you." Kiara smiled.

Hank smiled back. "I would like to talk to you about something. Can we meet after school?"

"Of course," Kiara replied.

Kiara sat in all of her classes, listening to the teachers, but the entire time she could not focus. One of her teachers even noticed and said, "Kiara, are you here with us today? Your mind seems to be somewhere else."

Kiara replied, "Yes, ma'am. I am right here with you right now." That was something her dad would teach his students to say at the dojo.

When they were daydreaming or not focused in class, Kiara remembered her dad asking the class, "How do we focus?"

The class would respond loudly, "Focus your mind, focus your heart, and focus your body. Shihan!"

This was a great way for Shihan to get everyone on the same page and focused entirely on him when he taught. Kiara pushed her imagination aside and started to focus on the class again. But all she could think about was what Hank had spoken about. Her imagination was getting the most of her. She remembered how Hank's dad's eyes did that flash of red thing when she saw him. She was suspicious and very curious about why that happened.

Before she knew it, the bell that signaled the end of the school day rang. Trying to look cool, she gathered her books, put them in her backpack, and started for the door. She was moving with a quicker step than usual, all while trying not to look too anxious.

CHAPTER THIRTEEN

The Conversation

Kiara made her way through the halls and saw Merrick, Teal, and Cody at their lockers. She walked right up to them and said, "I will catch up with you guys later. Remember, Hank had something he wanted to talk to me about."

Cody quickly said, "We should go with you. I don't trust that guy."

The other two boys said, "Yeah."

"Don't worry guys. I am a big girl. I can handle Hank. Plus, I trust in my heart that he is a great kid. He just needs some good friends."

Kiara was off and made her way around the corner to where Hank's locker was, and she saw him there. She walked up to him.

"Hey, what's up?"

"Let's walk and talk, because I can't go outside. My dad will be waiting there."

"Okay," Kiara said as they started walking down the hallway.

"So, Kiara, you may have noticed that my dad is not the kindest of people."

Kiara just looked at Hank without saying a word.

"Yeah, the weird thing, Kiara, is he wasn't always like that. Like your dad, he ran a martial art school and was a really cool guy, always looking out for his students. I think your dad and my dad were friends."

"Really?"

"Yes, Kiara. That is what is weird. It almost seems like my dad isn't my dad anymore."

"Wow that is strange." Kiara said with a slight squeak in her voice.

Hank replied, "Okay, thanks for listening. You have always been nice to me, even when I was not being so nice to others. Thank you for that. It has helped me change the way I acted. Everyone needs a friend, even jerks like me." He laughed softly.

"You are not a jerk, Hank. You are a good guy. I will always be there for you."

Kiara turned down the hall and started to leave. She quickly looked back and said, "Remember, Hank, the boys and I are here for you. Text me if you have any questions or want to chat. You have my number."

In a flash, she was on her bike, started pedaling away, and was on her way home. She then turned back and said, "Remember, Hank, me and the boys are here for you."

Before she knew it, the boys were right behind her. They never let her out of their sight, even though she asked them to trust her. They were tasked with always protecting her.

CHAPTER FOURTEEN

The Text Message That Changed Everything

Kiara had just finished her homework after a long training session at the dojo with her dad. It was an especially fun class because Kiara started to use her powers without anyone knowing. During the class, she was sparring, and in her mind, she imagined a force field around her. Every time a person tried to hit her, it seemed like she moved out of the way without any effort whatsoever.

The students she was sparring with, didn't seem to notice it, because Kiara was quite quick anyway. But this time she used her newly found powers and was able to evade her opponents with little to no effort whatsoever.

Kiara thought to herself, *this will certainly help if ever confronted by a violent opponent.* She was happy to see how it worked and how she could use it.

The minute she got home, she immediately started her homework. Her dad always said he never had to ask her to do it. She did it without ever being asked. She then immediately started cooking. Tonight was going to be a quick, easy meal. Both she and her dad were tired, so she started to boil water to cook spaghetti and took out her homemade pasta sauce from the refrigerator.

Later that night, Kiara was in her room texting when she saw a message come in from Hank.

Hank typed: "Kiara, I have been thinking about what you were saying, and I wanted to tell you something that is happening that is really weird. It isn't a new thing, but it has been happening for about a year."

Kiara replied, "Yeah, tell me about it. I would love to hear."

Hank: "Well, when you guys came by my house the other day, you saw my dad yelling at me."

Kiara: "Yeah?"

Hank: "Well, he was really angry and has been this way for about a year now. The weird thing is he was always the most patient, loving, and caring father. I never really gave it much thought, but ever since my mom left, I thought he was just bitter."

Kiara: "Hey, I know how it is to not have your mom around. Do you hear from your mom?"

Hank: "No, not really. She has a new family and really has nothing to do with me. But my dad is not nice to her either. In fact, she used to say, 'You are changing so much,' and said that is why she left."

Kiara: "Yeah, I can understand that. So what is your dad doing?"

Hank: "Well, he is always upset about something, but not in a normal way. He seems to always look for trouble. He always finds someone to be mad at. He is always angry. He also spends more and more time at that warehouse too."

Kiara: "What warehouse?"

Hank: "The warehouse where he teaches martial arts. It is more of a secret place, a hidden dojo. He also teaches all the troublemakers at school or in town and criminals too. He makes me go and makes me hurt people too. I think that is why I was picking on that kid in school. I don't like it and do not like how I feel when I do it."

Kiara: "Can I ask you a question? Does he change in any way when he acts like that?"

Kiara was fishing for a way to ask him about his dad's eyes and how they flashed red.

Hank: "Well, yeah. It seems that when he is in that mood, his eyes seem to glow in a weird red color. Then the other thing is when he is not there and at home, sometimes he just sits there and stares at the wall. He doesn't say anything to me and just sits for hours, almost like a zombie. LOL."

Kiara: "Well, that doesn't sound good. Would you mind if I brought this up with my dad and asked him? My dad and your dad used to be quite close. Would that be okay?"

Hank: "Yes, but please, please, please do not have him speak to my dad. Please."

Kiara: "Of course. We are Ninja. I will keep it a total secret. Thanks again for trusting me. I will ask him in the morning at breakfast."

CHAPTER FIFTEEN

Breakfast Couldn't Come Quick Enough

Kiara woke up without her alarm. She looked over at her clock and noticed she was up 30 minutes before her alarm had gone off. She immediately got up, jumped in the shower, and got ready for school. She was so early that her dad wasn't even at the table for breakfast, as he normally was. She rarely beat him down for breakfast. Her dad was always up, and the first thing he did was make his bed, get dressed, and come down to prepare Kiara's breakfast.

Kiara got down and decided she was so early that she would make her dad breakfast. She took out all the ingredients to make a vegetable omelet for herself with eggs and veggies. For her dad, because he was a vegan, someone who only eats vegetables, she made an all-vegetable burrito. It was sitting on the table as her dad came down.

"Woah, what is going on here? What has gotten into you?" he said.

"Nothing, Dad. I just wanted to make you a nice breakfast."

"Okay, kiddo."

They both sat down to eat.

Kiara said, "Dad, I have a question for you. Remember when you said to let you know if we see anything weird, or you mentioned something strange in the energy around us?"

"Yes, Kiara. Why? What did you feel?"

"Well, the other day, when the boys and I were going up to Master Macgregor's house to train, we saw Hank outside of his house as we rode by. His dad was yelling at him, and it appeared that he was about to hit him. Weren't you really good friends with his dad, Mr. Rast?"

"Yes, Kiara. We used to be really good friends back in the day. Then something changed. He got divorced, and we kind of stopped talking. Or should I say he stopped talking to me? I never knew why, but I couldn't get him to communicate."

"Dad, that is not the odd thing. When he was about to hit Hank, I pulled up on my bike and said hello to Hank. Mr. Rast wasn't too happy that I interrupted him. He told me to go away. But as I was leaving, his eyes seemed to change."

"Change, you say?"

"Yes. They flashed red, like in one of those alien movies, like there was something inside of him. It was weird. I saw it, and so did one of the boys. The next day, Hank came to school with a black eye. Then we spoke over text, and he said his dad has been acting very strange."

"Hmmm. That is not a good thing, Kiara."

"Dad, I promised Hank you would not approach his dad. He didn't want his dad to know he spoke to me. Can you please keep this a secret between us?"

"Of course, kiddo. But I will speak to Master Macgregor and see if we should be worried about this. Now let's finish up breakfast and get you to school."

"Okay, Dad. Hey, Dad."

"Yes, Kiara?"

"Dad, I love you. You're the best."

CHAPTER SIXTEEN

Tea Time

The next day, Shihan dropped off Kiara at school and drove up to meet with Master Macgregor. He arrived at his house and pulled into the long driveway leading up to the home. Master Macgregor was sitting on the patio with a hot cup of tea in his hand, and directly on a small table in front of him was a hot cup of green tea waiting for Shihan. Steam was pouring out the top of the Japanese-style tea cup.

"Ohayo gozaimasu," Master Macgregor stood and bowed. Shihan bowed back and repeated the phrase in English. "Good morning, Sennin." The two men sat with a smile.

"So, Kiara was telling me they had a run-in with Sensei Rast the other day. She told me that she and the boys were on their way up to train with you, and they saw him yelling at his son Hank. It appeared he was ready to hit him." Sennin MacGregor leaned forward a bit in his chair.

"There are two things that really bother me about this. First, Sensei Rast was always a calm and nice man. For all the years we traveled together competing and all the times we spent together as friends, he was never like this. I know we lost contact, and I thought it had to do with his wife, but now I am second-guessing myself. The second thing is Kiara said that she pulled up when he was yelling at Hank, and he ordered her to leave."

"Hmmm. That is very interesting. When I taught him, he was always a nice guy," Sennin MacGregor spoke softly.

"That is what I was thinking. But that is not the bad part. Kiara said that as she was about to leave, Sensei Rast looked at her, and his eyes flickered and flashed red. At first, she thought it was the light, but then she clearly saw that it was something from deep inside him."

"That could be very problematic. He is a very powerful man. Although he didn't really have any special powers like you and the four kids, he had high-level martial arts skills. Combine that with evil from another dimension, and we have the makings of something very, very bad." Sennin MacGregor took a sip of his tea and put his cup down.

"So, what is it that you suggest? Should I start to look into this? Try to find out what is going on? Kiara told me that Hank said his dad has been training a bunch of troubled kids and criminals at some warehouse in town for some months now. It may be worse than we originally thought. This is not a good sign." Shihan cleared his throat and took a sip of tea too.

"Whatever it is that you decide, just be very careful. We are not sure what we are dealing with," Master Macgregor said as the two men looked off into the mountains and had another sip of tea together.

CHAPTER SEVENTEEN

A Night Mission

Through the eyes of the binoculars, Shihan could see the warehouse filled with young teens and adults training in martial arts. There were about 30 to 35 of them training hard. They ranged in age from 13 up to adults. Shihan was lying on his stomach on top of a nearby building, with the binoculars resting on the ledge so no one could see his head popping up. This was a way for him to stay hidden in the shadows. After all, Shihan was a Ninja and taught Ninjutsu at his dojo, which is the art of the ninja.

He watched for a while as the students fought each other with weapons and struck each other. It seemed odd because they were hitting each other hard, yet they didn't seem to feel any pain at all. This was scary to Shihan. They didn't appear to be human, almost like robots.

All at once, the training stopped. Shihan couldn't hear clearly because he was far away, watching through the binoculars. The students ran to a long line and stood at attention. Mr. Rast, referred to as Sensei Rast, walked into view. He stood at the front of the line, yelling. Shihan zoomed in and saw that his face was angry.

The students stood without moving, not even to scratch or fidget. This was something Shihan often spoke about in his dojo. He called it extreme focus. In fact, he had a drill where he taught the students to touch the side of their head with their right hand and say, "Focus," then touch the other side of their head with their left and say, "Extreme Focus." Finally, they would push both hands out into a triangle and point forward, saying, "Laser Beam Focus." The kids loved this and memorized it.

He saw the students standing with that kind of laser beam focus, but one thing that was really scary was all of their eyes all were glowing red. They were like zombies. It was not normal.

Shihan uttered under his breath, "This is not of this world."

Then Shihan heard a footstep behind him and a crackle. He quickly turned and jumped up, preparing to defend himself. He thought there was no way they knew he was there. He turned quickly and noticed a fox walking up. He paused, lowered his hands, and dropped to his knee. The fox approached and transformed into a person.

"When did you learn that you could shape-shift?" Shihan asked.

Kiara looked up and said, "A few days ago while meditating. This is cool, Dad. I can literally turn into any animal I want. The bigger ones are much harder. So far, I have turned into an eagle, a fox, and a wolf. I tried to turn into a bear, but it didn't seem like I could do it."

"Well, the larger animals are definitely much more difficult. It took your mom much longer to figure that out."

"My mom? She was like me? Why didn't you tell me she was a shapeshifter like me?"

"Well, you never asked." Shihan giggled a little.

"Let's get out of here before someone notices us. Things are not good in Mr. Rast's little warehouse dojo. We are really not in a good spot right now. We are going to have to do something about this."

"Hey, kiddo, I worry about you, but you are a warrior. I have a mission for you. Can you turn into a bird or a mouse and make your way over to that warehouse to hear what is going on? Turn into something that is less noticeable, like a pigeon."

"You don't have to ask me twice. I love flying. Okay, I am off."

Like magic, a pigeon appeared in front of Shihan and immediately flew away. "That's my little shape-shifter," he smiled, though he was worried about her. He saw her fly into the rafters of the warehouse and land on top with the other pigeons. They didn't seem to notice her either.

Kiara sat at her perch and listened in as Sensei Rast taught his group of students. A larger man ran up from a different room and whispered in Mr. Rast's ear. Kiara could hear what he was saying.

"Sensei, I think we have found the location of the book. If we can get control of that book, we can finally start to really make our plan take action. If we can get the book with the spells, we can bring everyone from the other dimension into this one. If we do that, there will be nothing they can do to stop us. They will all be our slaves and have to work for us as we take full control of this planet," the large man said.

Kiara had heard enough. She flew away as both men looked up at her, but they didn't take much notice. Kiara was home in no time at all. As she was coming in for the landing on her front lawn, she transformed and continued walking to the front door.

CHAPTER EIGHTEEN

Training at Sennin MacGregor's Home

The next day was Saturday, and everyone was up at Master MacGregor's home for their late Saturday evening training class. The sun was starting to set, but they still had an hour or so of sunlight to train. Off in the distance, you could hear the waterfall flowing and beating down on the rocks. It echoed through the mountains and was a very relaxing sound.

The boys were training with Kiara on Taijutsu, which is empty-hand self-defense. They were on an outside deck that stood alone in the back corner of the yard. It was covered in Tatami mats, just like the ones in the dojo.

Kiara was surrounded by Teal, Merrick, and Cody, and they took turns attacking her with various moves. Kiara would spin and flip her opponents using techniques like Ippon Seoi-nage, the shoulder throw, or Omote Gyaku, the wrist lock throw. The boys were not pulling punches and attacked Kiara quickly and hard. She seemed to move with ease, and it looked like she barely touched them. She did all of this without using any magical skills whatsoever. After one boy was done, they switched, and the next opponent got in the middle, repeating the training exercise.

They continued like this for hours. To them, the workout was a game and fun. They didn't look at it as work. Tonight, though, there was another guest helping out. He was off to the side, coaching and encouraging the boys not to get lazy or sloppy. It was Renshi Ryan, who had come along with

Shihan. As Renshi coached and motivated the crew, he was off to the side shooting his bow and arrow. He loved archery and using the Japanese-style long bow.

Renshi Ryan was a marksman and also an amazing swordsman. As he coached, he shot without missing a beat. "Come on, guys, clean that move up. Move quicker, smoother. Remember, slow is smooth, and smooth is fast." He shot the cap off a plastic soda bottle with ease.

He then reloaded his arrow, notched it, and took a deep, relaxing breath to gain focus. Out of the corner of his eye, he released the arrow, and it hit dead center on the target, a bull's-eye. He turned to the boys and looked at them. Then he notched four arrows at once and pointed them at the kids.

They didn't seem to be paying attention. A weird smirk came over Renshi's face as he released the arrows. They were headed straight toward the four kids, or should we say the Four Kings. Without even seeing it, they all performed gymnastic moves and ended up catching the arrows.

Renshi smiled. "Nicely done. You are really starting to develop what we call laser beam focus. You are growing so powerful."

Shihan sat on the porch of the house, watching with Sennin MacGregor. They had their favorite tea in hand and continued to discuss what had been developing and what he and Kiara had seen at the warehouse.

CHAPTER NINETEEN

Meeting of the Masters

"**N**ow is the time that we have to protect the book. On our last adventure, we hid it in that mountain, in the Ice Cave in Ellenville, N.Y. We have to get it and keep it safe," Shihan spoke a little above a whisper.

"Do you think it makes sense to take it out of hiding and bring it back into the world? I think it is safe behind the wall of spells in its secret hiding place. I don't think even the best of the best could get past that," Master MacGregor whispered back as he watched the kids train their hearts out.

"I know, but I think the world wants us to take it out. We have Kings to protect it. How do you think we got so lucky to have kids like that, with these special powers, ready to help us save the world once again? I think they are the nature's plan of protecting the book."

"I have to be honest. It has a lot to do with you, Shihan. You have taken these children since they were babies and trained them in the art of Ninjutsu at your school. Yes, you knew in your heart that these were very special kids out of thousands, but you chose right."

"Yeah, all I did was look for the most dedicated, and yes, I could feel something about them that I knew made them special," Shihan smiled.

"So do you feel we should keep the book hidden or take it out of hiding?" Master MacGregor looked over at the boys as they attacked Kiara one more time, with Renshi watching. All at once, they grabbed Kiara from all sides. She seemed to be caught, and the boys held her in place. She struggled a bit, but a smile came over her face. With a snap, she was done, and the boys all fell into each other. Cody, Merrick, and Teal bounced off each other as a little mouse scurried across the outside dojo mats.

"Hey, that's not fair," they all said at once. Master MacGregor replied with a look and a shake of his head. He looked at Shihan. "Like mother, like daughter." Shihan smiled as they leaned in to whisper even lower this time.

CHAPTER TWENTY

The Warehouse

Sensei Rast stood in front of his students and warriors. "Our mission begins tomorrow. Do you understand?" The students replied all at once, "Ooos!" loudly, which is a show of respect and agreement in the martial art of Karate.

"Go home, and tomorrow you will start with our plan of causing as much chaos as possible, starting with the town. Do you understand?" "Yes, Sir!" they all yelled together.

A man came out of the shadows and walked forward toward Sensei Rast. For the first time, his face was visible, and Sensei Rast bowed deeply, mostly out of fear, not respect. It was Master Hatanaka from their last adventure.

Master Hatanaka said, "You brought me back even more powerful than I was before, but we need to join our forces to make sure that this time we are not overtaken or beaten by the Three Kings and Master MacGregor's group. Is that understood?"

"Yes, sir," replied Sensei Rast with a deep bow of respect.

CHAPTER TWENTY-ONE

Chaos

The day started off like any other day. It was a quiet morning, and Kiara woke up, sat up, and stretched her arms. She quickly hopped out of bed and made her way downstairs from her bedroom. She saw her dad sitting at the island in their kitchen, having a cup of tea. He was watching the news on the TV.

He turned as Kiara walked into the kitchen. She could tell by the look on his face that something just wasn't right.

"What's wrong, Dad? What is going on?"

"Hey, kiddo, it is all starting just like we thought. They are going to cause as much damage and mayhem as they can to create a diversion and chaos in our small town. There are house fires raging everywhere and the police and fire fighters are stretched thin. They are blaming it on a few arsons but the news is saying they have no idea who is starting these fires. You and I both know who is doing this and we have to act quick or many lives and our entire community is in danger."

"Reach out to the boys and Renshi and tell them to meet us at the dojo in one hour and to bring their tools. I have some other people I need to reach out to, but I swore that I would never bother them again. This is not going away, and it won't be easy. I have to get all the help we can. I think it is time that I ask you, Kiara, to help me gather all the animals, and I will get in contact with the Sennin Warriors: Master Tora, the Cheetah; Master

Fukurou, the Owl; Master Kitsune, the Fox. Also, our friends the Eagle, Bear, and Wolf, Washii, Kuma and Okami. Kiara, it will be your job to get all the animals on the same page from this world. They do not have powers other than their animal abilities, but they can certainly help us fight these evil forces."

"Let's go, kiddo," Shihan said.

"Yes, Dad. I will go out to the woods and start communicating with our friends," Kiara replied.

CHAPTER TWENTY-TWO

Protecting the Book

"What can we do to protect the book?" Shihan asked Kiara.

"Dad, we can go to the ice cave and fortify the spell even more, give it more strength so that no one can get through to get it. I know we can do it if we work together."

Shihan nodded in approval and said, "Okay, let's go do that now. There is no time to waste."

They jumped into their vehicle and drove up to the Ice Caves. When they got there, they parked and began an almost one-hour walk up to the entrance. The path was long and winding, filled with many obstacles and areas to climb. However, there were many man-made bridges and handrails along the dangerous areas.

Once inside, they made their way through a maze of twists, turns, and narrow paths within the cave. When they arrived at the spot where the tour normally ended for sightseers, they performed an incantation (spell) toward the area where the book was hidden.

They immediately noticed that someone had beaten them there and attempted to break through the spell to get into the book's hiding place. The good news was that the spell held, but Shihan said, "Kiara, I know we can fortify the spell and make it stronger, and I am glad that it held the first time. But I don't think we should allow them to come back and try again."

"Yes, I was thinking the same thing. They don't quit easily and who knows who they have on their side to help them get the book and use it with bad intentions." Kiara said without taking a breath.

Shihan started an incantation spell and asked Kiara to join in. She already knew the spell, so she easily joined. After a few minutes, a swirling bit of wind started to spin, and the cave wall opened. Sitting in front of them was the book on a stand, safely out of harm's way.

Shihan walked up and grabbed the book, and he and Kiara walked out. They left with extreme caution and kept their eyes open at every turn. Finally, they made it to their car and were quickly en route to Master Macgregor's house.

When they finally arrived at the house, Kiara broke the silence. "Dad, why don't we go up to the waterfalls? I have a perfect place to hide the book."

"Okay, kiddo, let's do that. I trust you."

They grabbed the book and started walking through the woods. Shihan followed close behind Kiara. The sound of crashing water grew louder and louder as they got closer. Soon they were there.

Kiara spoke softly. "Dad, I can use my powers to open up the rocks within the waterfall, and we can hide the book there."

"Okay, good idea. Let's do that."

Kiara began to chant, and the waterfall seemed to stop as the rocks beneath it moved out of the way, opening up another small cave. Shihan walked over, placed the book inside the small opening, and stepped back. With a wave of her hand, Kiara closed the cave, and the water began to flow over it again.

"Now it is time to get to the dojo. We have class soon, and we have to work on our powers more."

Kiara spoke again. "I want to do one more thing." She called out to all the animals, and they started to appear one by one. There was a group of animals: wolves, bears, owls, foxes, a cheetah, and one eagle. The cheetah was definitely not from around this area.

They all sat and listened as Kiara said, "We need you to watch over this book. If anyone comes looking, do what you have to do to protect it. Please let me know if anything happens or anything unusual goes on."

The animals seemed to listen and then walked away, but the eagle screeched and flew right toward Kiara, landing gently on her arm without letting its talons cut her. Kiara leaned over and spoke into the eagle's ear.

Shihan asked, "What did you tell the Washii (eagle)?"

Kiara replied, "That wasn't just an eagle. That was Mom in her animal form."

CHAPTER TWENTY-THREE

Training Like a Ninja at the Dojo

The dojo was full of energy, with many different groups practicing their martial arts skills. A variety of instructors led the groups as they all practiced different techniques. Ever so often, they would change the positioning of the groups, and then that group would change what they were practicing.

It seemed the focus was all on Taijutsu, self-defense training. Students were paired up, practicing techniques just taught to them by the teacher in charge of their group. Others were practicing with their partners on their own, training the moves they had already learned to master them.

One of the kids said, "Sumimasen, Sensei (excuse me)."

The main instructor stopped the entire room by yelling, "Yame," which means to stop. The teacher then said, "Jameson, you have a question? Ask me now."

Young Jameson said, "Sensei, why do we practice this stuff over and over again? I am getting bored. I want to learn newer, cooler stuff."

The sensei responded with a comment he had heard Shihan Allie say many times. "If you are getting bored, then you are obviously missing the lesson. Repetition is not something that should make you bored; it should excite you. It is more of a gift than something that should make you less motivated. Think about this: a baseball player has thousands of strikeouts in their career. They never quit or say the game is boring, now do they?"

The kids replied loudly, "No, sir!" all at once.

The instructor asked, "Then why do they keep going? Why don't they quit or get bored? I will tell you why. Because if they strike out twenty-five times out of a hundred, then they are considered amazing. Reggie Jackson, one of the all-time great baseball players, struck out 2,597 times in his 11,418 at-bats."

The students stood quietly, waiting for the answer. "Mr. Jackson had 2,597 career strikeouts, but he also had 563 home runs, which ranked him fourteenth of all time. He also had 2,584 hits in his career. He was a 14-time All-Star and won the American League MVP award in 1973. Does that help put boredom in perspective?"

The student said, "Hai, Sensei."

They all continued training, but even harder than before.

Shihan stepped out onto the mat. One student yelled out, "Yame!" The class stopped what they were doing and faced Shihan. They all turned, bowed, and said, "Onegaishimasu (please teach me)."

Shihan started talking to a group of leadership members who were also part of his demonstration team. He spoke to them about the pending battle that was about to take place between good and evil. He mentioned what was happening, instructed them, and told them they needed to get themselves prepared. They all agreed and bowed respectfully. Then they got back to sweating and training as hard as ever to prepare for the battle.

CHAPTER TWENTY-FOUR

Getting Ready for the Battle

Shihan woke early. It was 3:30 a.m. and still dark outside. He walked into Kiara's room and sat softly on the bed. Before waking her, he stared at her for a moment with a smile on his face. He was filled with pride but also worry because what was about to happen was both dangerous and frightening. He didn't want to put his daughter in harm's way.

He reached over, brushed Kiara's long hair out of her face, and said, "It's time to wake up, kiddo."

"Five more minutes, please, Dad."

Shihan sat quietly and gave her the five minutes she asked for. Normally, he would have said, "I will race you downstairs for breakfast." That usually made Kiara jump out of bed and run to her favorite seat in the kitchen. Shihan just smiled and sat patiently. He knew that this was going to be an incredibly difficult day for all of them.

When the five minutes on her alarm clock passed, he said, "Okay, you got your five minutes. Now it's time to wake up and get ready. Please don't make me race you downstairs."

She lifted her head, ready to run, then smiled, realizing what he was doing. "Dad, you almost had me there. Okay, I'll be down in a few minutes. Let me get dressed and ready to go."

Shihan left the room and walked down the stairs. It was early for breakfast, so he packed a bag filled with snacks and food that could keep them fed throughout the day. Within a few minutes, Kiara came down the steps filled with energy and excitement. He handed her the bag and said, "You ready?"

She nodded as they walked out the door.

They got into the car and headed toward Master MacGregor's house in the mountains. It was about a twenty-minute drive, and they were a bit quite on the ride. As they approached the long, winding driveway, they saw a large group of people assembled in the field. This group was filled with students from Shihan's dojo, other martial artists, and a large gathering of animals; eagles, bears, wolves, foxes, owls, and one rather large, muscular cheetah standing upright on his rear legs. He appeared to be talking to the rest of the animals, giving them some sort of pep talk. There were about forty animals in total and another forty people.

Shihan's vehicle slowed down. He put the car in park, and both he and Kiara stepped out. One of the students, named Caleb, noticed and yelled, "Yame (stop)! Present yourself to Shihan and bow!"

Caleb loved to do this and never missed a chance, whether in the dojo or outside. The group listened to Caleb and stopped what they were doing. They snapped to attention, turned, and faced Shihan and Kiara.

"Shisei o tadaste! Shihan and Sensei Kiara ni rei!"

This meant, *present yourself to Shihan and Kiara*, and everyone bowed and said, "Onegaishimasu."

CHAPTER TWENTY-FIVE

Before the Battle

Shihan and Kiara walked up to the group of students and warriors and began to speak. "Thank you for coming today. This is probably one of the most important things you can be involved with in your lifetime." He turned to the group of animals. "Sennin, thank you for coming." He bowed. "Your presence means the world to me, and of course your strength and fighting ability will make all the difference. Without you I don't know if we could do it, so thank you." He bowed again. They all went down on one knee in a bow called Jinchu Rei. They nodded their heads downward in a sign of loyalty and approval.

"We are going to be meeting at Sensei Rast's warehouse. They are meeting there at 6 a.m. We can confront them there and hopefully talk some sense into them, but I don't think that they will listen to reasoning or kind words. So be prepared for battle. Are you all ready?"

The group replied in a strong, powerful tone, "Hai, Shihan."

They all bowed and moved to their vehicles, and the animals scurried off into the woods. The birds of prey took to the sky to get there ahead of time to look over the warehouse. It seemed like a tense twenty or so minutes when Shihan and his team pulled off on a dirt road away from the warehouse. They all started to gather and Shihan gave them one last pep talk.

Back in the warehouse, Sensei Rast was yelling at his followers and students as they stood in perfectly organized lines, just like you would see in a military movie. "Do you understand this is our last chance?" Rast yelled. The students stayed quiet and stood still. "I need that book and I need to eliminate the threat of Shihan, Master MacGregor, and Renshi and his students. We cannot have them around to protect this world and the book. They are the only thing that stands between us and winning the battle to control the planet."

Rast was obviously very worked up and angry. He felt that he should have been in control all these years and received the recognition he deserved, but Shihan had the respect of the community and his students.

The eagles and owls stood on a tree branch not too far from the warehouse so they could see and hear everything that was going on. Rast quickly turned, looked up into the sky, and noticed them on the branches. "You don't think I know who you are," he yelled at the sennin. "I am aware you are watching over us. So tell Shihan and his people that if they continue to come we will destroy them and then there will be no chance of survival for the world as you know it. We will be in charge."

The eagle and owl flew off and in seconds landed on Kiara's and Shihan's shoulders and spoke in human words. "Shihan and Sensei," the eagle said, "They know we are here and on our way. They are prepared for us and there is a rather large group of them."

Shihan replied, "What do you think we should do?"

Kiara interrupted. "Dad, I think I have an idea that would save many people from getting hurt. I think it will be something that Sensei Rast has wanted for years and I think his ego will not stop him from accepting."

"Go ahead, Kiara, I am all ears," Shihan said.

"I think that if we go into a full battle many people will be injured. I think if we challenge Sensei Rast his pride will get the best of him and we can get him to accept. I suggest picking the best of our students to do a competition and fight in a fair tournament. This would be a full-contact fight, but it would be five of our best against five of his. What do you think?"

Shihan put his hand on his chin and thought for a minute. "Kiddo, you are a genius. I love the idea." The students agreed with Kiara.

"Why don't we send Washii and Fukuro, the eagle and owl, to present our challenge? If they win, we step aside and they do what they want, but if we win, they will agree to stop the madness and stop trying to take over the world and control it."

Shihan turned to Washii and Fukuro and nodded. The two birds of prey were in flight within seconds on their way back to the warehouse.

CHAPTER TWENTY-SIX

The Offer

Sensei Rast was preparing his warriors for the final battle in his mind. All he could think of was taking control of the planet. He knew once he had the book, there would be no stopping him. He did worry, though, that if Shihan, his students, and the team of sennin could stop him right in his tracks, he would be exiled.

He was yelling out commands as his students fought. Some used weapons like the yari (long staff and spear), the naginata (long staff with a sword attached), katana (swords), nunchaku, and some archers with bow and arrows known as yumi and ya.

It was obvious that Sensei Rast was not a kind person. He didn't care about the safety of his students. To him they were just warriors in a battle. All he cared about was winning, partially so he could lead the world, but the other reason was more about ego.

In the middle of practice, while Sensei Rast was yelling at his students, he noticed Fukuro and Washii flying above his head. They circled overhead and landed on a box in front of Sensei Rast. He immediately yelled out, "Yame." His warriors immediately stopped and snapped to attention with a clap on their hips. The snap sounded like thunder echoing through the warehouse.

"Well, well, what do we have here, my little friends Washii and Fukuro. Shihan's most trusted friends." The archers raised their bows, notched arrows, and pointed them directly at the two birds of prey. "Do not shoot those arrows. Lower your bows," he yelled.

In a deep booming voice that no one would have expected from a bird that size, Washii spoke. "Sensei," he said as he nodded his head, "you and I have not seen each other in quite some time. I know you remember me and who I am. I know there is a battle about to start of epic proportions. However, before all of these young amazing people who are under your spell get hurt, we have a challenge for you."

Sensei Rast smirked. "Oh yeah, what might that be?"

Washii replied, "I know you have a martial arts code and will not turn down an honorable challenge. I know you want to win badly enough, so we challenge you to a tournament of martial arts." Sensei Rast turned, looked at his warriors, and then looked back.

"I am listening. What is it you are about to offer to seal your destiny?"

Washii replied, "It is simple. You take your best five people and put them up against our five best for a battle. No rules, just pure fighting with either weapons or none. It is your choice. That is, if you have five people that could even compare to the ability of Shihan's students." He taunted Sensei Rast.

You could see Sensei Rast's jaw tighten as he ground his teeth together. He was listening but also quite tense and didn't like that this was what they were offering. "Of course you could say no. I would understand if you felt your five best didn't stand a chance against Shihan's warriors."

"Shut up!" Sensei Rast yelled. He was clearly annoyed at the challenge and felt compelled to take it. "My five best against yours, that is easy." He laughed. "You tell me when and where."

Washii replied, "Tomorrow morning at dawn is fine. We can do it right here in your dojo. The rules are there are NO rules. However, you must agree that if you lose you go away forever, leave this world, and stop trying to take it over. You must promise with the code of martial arts to agree."

Sensei Rast thought for a while. You could see his jaw tightening and loosening when one of his men leaned over and whispered into his ear, "You don't have to play by the rules. This is our war." Sensei Rast turned and slapped the man hard in the face.

"This is not how warriors battle. We fight with a code of honor. It doesn't matter what the battle is about, we have a martial code."

Sensei Rast turned to Washii and Fukuro, bowed, and said angrily, "Challenge accepted. See you back here tomorrow at dawn."

CHAPTER TWENTY-SEVEN

The Choosing

The morning came quickly and the sun started to rise. Shihan's warriors were all at Sensei Rast's warehouse dojo earlier than they were expected. On one side stood Sensei Rast in front of his warriors and on the other side stood Shihan's warriors. They all stood at perfect attention. They almost looked like statues.

Shihan walked to the center, up to the tatami mats, took off his shoes, bowed, and stepped forward. Sensei Rast did the same. They met face to face for the first time in a very long time.

"This reminds me of the old days, when we used to fight in the dojo. The only thing back then was we were friends," Shihan said.

"Yes, that is true. You were always Master MacGregor's favorite and he was always easy on you." You could tell there was still bad blood there.

"I remember it differently, my old seito (student). I was your sempai (big brother) and you were always a little jealous. I always treated you just like a little brother. Not sure where and why you changed."

"Let's get on with this. Bring up your five warriors," Rast said.

Shihan turned toward his people and called out the names. First was Renshi, then he called Cody, Merrick, and Teal. "That is only four, you need one more."

"I know how to count, Rast." He then called out, "Kiara."

"Ah, you are going to put your daughter in harm's way. I knew you weren't that smart." Shihan knew it was dangerous, but he also knew Kiara was strong and had the skills and, moreover, had the power of his mother, the animals, and her special abilities on her side. All five warriors walked up.

Sensei Rast yelled, "My five warriors, join us up front." They were ready and walked up and stood in front of Shihan's team.

"How do you want to do this, all at once or individual matches?" Shihan asked.

"Let's do this one at a time so I can watch each one of my members beat yours. It will be that much more pleasurable for my students and me," Rast replied.

Shihan bowed and walked back with his students following closely behind him.

CHAPTER TWENTY-EIGHT

The Battle

Match One:

Both teams stepped back. Shihan called up Cody. Cody stepped up to the mat lines and stood ready. Sensei Rast called up his first warrior, a very muscular, taller student with black hair and a scruffy beard. They called him Dante. He seemed older than Cody by about five years. Cody just stood still, waiting. The two men looked at each other. Akuma commanded, "Bow." The two men bowed, and then he said, "Hajime.".

Cody and Dante squared off and stepped back into their stances. The fight began. Dante came in with a flurry of punches and kicks. Cody backed up, blocking every move. On the last punch, Cody grabbed Dante's hand and spun him around in a technique called the Island, and then with his forearm he hit him in the chest, knocking him to the ground. When Dante hit the ground, Cody punched him in the stomach. Dante groaned in pain. The judge, Akuma, raised his hand reluctantly and loudly said, "Point!" It was 1-0 in favor of Cody. Cody smiled at Dante and jumped back into his fighting stance.

When Dante stood up, he was obviously angry. He slapped the mat and immediately charged at Cody with both hands out to grab or push him. Cody weaved one hand in and one out, circling under Dante's arm and stepped in front in what is known as Ganseki Nage, or Stone Throw, and threw him again. This time Dante fell real hard, and you could see he was physically in pain. Cody stood over him and just looked into his eyes.

Dante pulled himself into a back roll and stood up. He then came at Cody again with a flurry of punches and kicks, with a spinning hook kick he hit Cody right in the face. Cody spun in a circle and hit the mat. Akuma pointed in Dante's direction and called point.

It was 2-1 in Cody's favor.

The two men, a little wobbly, stood in front of each other and crossed their lead hands as the judge held onto them. Dante and Cody looked over at their teachers. The judge released their hands, and with a lightning-fast back fist, Cody hit Dante in the face, knocking him backward. The match was over. Akuma pointed to Cody. "Winner."

Match Two:

The judge looked toward Sensei Rast and called out his next fighter, "Kuchiku-kan, the Destroyer." This fighter was an older gentleman in his late thirties. Shihan called out, "Renshi Ryan, koko ni kitte kudasai (please come here)."

Renshi spoke loudly, "Hai, Shihan."

Both men faced each other. Renshi looked at his opponent and gave a humble bow. The opponent barely nodded and smirked. The referee put his hand between the two men, raised it up, and said, "Hajime."

Both men circled each other, cautious of the other's first move. The Destroyer charged toward Renshi with a flurry of attacks. Renshi quickly deflected the attacks and moved side to side, avoiding every move. Not one of them hit him. With a quick twist of his arm, he circled Kuchiku-kan's arm, locked him up, and turned him facedown. Stepping in front of his legs, he flipped him to the ground. Renshi finished with a punch with just enough power to the stomach to knock the wind out of him.

Kuchiku-kan got up quickly, but angrily, and immediately charged at Renshi again. The judge had to get in between them to stop them and call the point. He pushed both opponents back and pointed in Renshi's direction. "Point!" he yelled. It was 1-0.

Kuchiku-kan charged and jumped in the air with a flying side kick aimed at Renshi's head. Renshi slid out of the way with a side roll and evaded the attack. Renshi then delivered a spinning hook kick to his head as the Destroyer fell to the ground. The referee ran in, stopped the fight, and called it. "2-0, next point wins."

Kuchiku-kan was visibly shaken but still very angry. He was letting his anger get the best of him. He charged Renshi again and was able to grab him on both sides of his uniform. Renshi smiled because close-quarter grappling was his favorite thing to practice.

Renshi grabbed his arms and locked them in as he lay back, putting his feet in Kuchiku-kan's hip joints and pulled him on top, kicking up with his feet and flipping him over. This was known as a monkey flip. Renshi pulled himself on top of his opponent and finished with a submission arm bar until Kuchiku-kan tapped out, giving up. The fight was finished by submission.

Both men stood up and faced each other. Reluctantly, the referee pointed in Renshi's direction and said, "Winner."

Sensei Rast was visibly annoyed. He turned toward his fighters.

Match Three:

This time it was a woman in her twenties named Nicole. Nicole came running in and stopped at the line. Shihan looked over at Kiara and nodded his head. She did a front roll and stood up at the line. Sensei Rast grabbed a Naginata. This was a bow staff with a wooden sword on the end; it wasn't the bladed version. Of course, the real one was made of razor-sharp steel.

Merrick came running up and handed Kiara her Naginata. They both bowed in a special bow called Jinchu Rei, with one knee on the ground.

This bow was reserved for real battles. Both opponents bowed to each other with respect. Nicole knew Kiara because they had competed against each other in tournaments many times before and had mutual respect for each other. Nicole knew, however, that she needed to win, or she would pay the price and have to deal with Sensei Rast's temper.

They stood up, weapons in hand, and clicked their weapons together as they stepped back and began circling each other cautiously. Both girls started doing what was known as a reverse figure-eight and got close enough to start clashing weapons. Nicole tried her best to knock the Naginata out of Kiara's hands, but Kiara anticipated the move and parried it out of the way in a half circle. Once she did that, it left Nicole's right leg wide open as she cut down. Nicole's reflexes were quick; she lifted her leg and avoided the strike.

Just then, Kiara saw Nicole's eyes flash red. She was obviously under some sort of spell and started moving extra fast. Kiara struggled to keep up, and Nicole was able to sweep both of Kiara's feet out from under her. Instead of letting her stand, Nicole used the butt end of the weapon to hit Kiara in the head. Kiara was dazed and a little dizzy. As Kiara staggered to stand, Nicole swung again at her head, but Kiara managed to avoid it. Just then, Kiara's mom appeared in the distance, but only Kiara could see her. Kiara smiled and stepped back, shaking her head and the dizziness..

Nicole and Kiara crossed their weapons again. The referee said, "1-0," while pointing at Nicole. He then said, "Hajime." Nicole started again and came in with a flurry of strikes, but this time Kiara stood her ground. She used the butt end of the weapon to strike Nicole in the stomach. Nicole fell back, falling to one knee. The referee pointed in Kiara's direction. "Point." The score was 1-1, tie score.

Kiara waited in a defensive stance while Nicole charged again with attack after attack. Kiara evaded and blocked, waiting until another opening appeared. She used the same move and hit Nicole in the stomach again, making her fall to her knee once more. The judge awarded Kiara another point.

The score was 2-1 in Kiara's favor. This time, when they squared off, Kiara attacked with her own strikes and landed one right on Nicole's leg. The referee yelled, "Yame!" He then awarded the point to Kiara. The final score was 3-1. Nicole had a hard time getting to her feet because her leg was injured.

Kiara stood in attention stance and bowed to Nicole, then turned toward her dad and bowed with a smile on her face. Shihan smiled back and bowed.

Match Four:

The referee yelled, "Next match, send in your competitors." Shihan looked at Teal. Teal was a strong grappler and fighter, able to handle any style. He dove rolling into the center and hit his mark, waiting to see who Sensei Rast would pick. The crowd parted as a huge six-foot-tall, muscular man walked through. He had a patch over one eye and tattoos all over his body, neck, and face.

Sensei Rast's students were visibly excited to see this huge man. They started chanting, "Patch, Patch, Patch." He got the nickname because of the patch on his eye. He hit his mark, stopped, and smirked at Teal. Teal did not show any sign of nervousness and held a steady stare, though inside he felt uneasy. Shihan always taught his students to never show worry or fear. He called it having a stone face; showing no emotions.

The man smirked and laughed, saying in a deep, raspy voice, "This is going to be a piece of cake."

The referee spoke loudly, "Bow to each other!" Both competitors bowed. Before the referee could say start, the big man strongly shoved Teal back. Teal went with the push and rolled on the ground, right up to his feet. The man was upset that his power didn't affect him. He charged forward with a series of punches and kicks, but Teal slipped each one with ease using his Tai Sabaki, or body movement, which they practiced regularly at the dojo.

The man committed to a punch with all his power. Teal blocked it and used it to wrist-lock the man, flipping him onto his back. He immediately stood up, punching the floor in anger. The referee stepped between them.

He put his hands up and pushed them away from each other, but the big man shoved him back and attacked Teal again. As the man came in with a left-right punch combination, Teal blocked and jumped into the air, kicking him with both legs, hitting him square in the chest. Normally, a kick like this would knock someone off their feet, but the man stood his ground; he was very strong. Teal bounced off and fell to the ground in a back fall, hitting the floor. Teal bounced right back up with a Kip-Up, a gymnastic move where the body flips back to its feet using the hands and arching the body. The referee did not call a point, even though it hit the big man. That was two points not called. The referee was obviously leaning toward Sensei Rast's team.

The man charged again with his hands down. Teal jumped high in the air, spinning, and performed a hook kick. He hit the huge man square in the jaw. The man spun to the floor and did not move. He was knocked out cold. The match was over, and Teal was the winner. That made four wins for Shihan and zero for Sensei Rast.

Sensei Rast raised his hand and said, "Yame." He called a time-out and walked to the front of the crowd and his students.

"This is boring me. Why don't we make the next match more interesting? Why don't we do a multiple-opponent fight with no rules? Why don't you and I fight alongside our last fighters? That is, if you are not afraid. Let's say winner takes all."

Shihan looked back at Merrick, who nodded in approval. Shihan then looked at Sensei Rast. "Are you sure you will admit defeat and let this battle go if we win?" Sensei Rast bowed slowly, showing he still had a little respect left for Shihan. Shihan nodded in approval and walked back to Merrick. They started to work on a strategy.

CHAPTER TWENTY-NINE

The Final Match

Shihan talked to his team while Sensei Rast was speaking to his last team member. They both realized this was for the win. No matter how well Shihan's team did in the past few matches, they were forfeiting those wins for the last match. It was winner-takes-all. You could feel the tension in the air. Both teams and all of their students were on the edge of their seats.

Sensei Rast walked to the middle and placed down three weapons: a Katana (sword), a pair of Kama (sickles chained together), and a six-foot-long Bo Staff. He said whoever got to these weapons could use them. Shihan nodded in approval.

The referee walked to the center of the lines and said, "All fighters up." He then went over the agreement with both sides. The final winners of this match would take it all. This was it. No questions, no arguing. This would put an end to the battle once and for all, for the planet.

He pointed to Shihan and Merrick and asked, "Are you ready?" They both bowed. He then pointed to Sensei Rast's side and asked, "Are you ready?" They bowed back. He then yelled, "Then let the fights begin!"

Both sides charged for the weapons. Shihan and Sensei Rast stood there, staring at each other and circling. Merrick rolled in quickly, but Sensei Rast's team beat him to the Bo Staff, so Merrick grabbed the Katana. It was Bo versus Sword. Immediately, there was a flurry of moves from both

Merrick and his opponent. They were both blocking, moving, and doing their best not to get hit. Sensei Rast and Shihan continued to circle each other until Rast came in with a one-two punch and front kick combination. Shihan easily blocked it and countered with a spinning side kick to Rast's stomach, pushing him back three feet. In this match, no points were being called; it was whoever was left standing.

Merrick cut with the Katana and chopped the Bo in half, but the opponent started using it as two separate weapons, just like a pair of Escrima sticks. He came in with a figure-eight type move, and Merrick kept blocking and moving. He then knocked one stick out of his opponent's hand and held the sword two inches from his head. The man submitted and gave up, walking out of the arena. Merrick also stepped aside. Remaining were Shihan versus Sensei Rast.

Just then, one of Sensei Rast's students broke the rules and came rolling in, grabbing the Kama and getting between Shihan and Rast. He tried to attack Shihan, but in a flash, Merrick and Teal joined in and blocked the attacks. Sensei Rast and Shihan began to grapple, holding onto each other's uniforms. Sensei Rast attempted to sweep Shihan, but he countered with a defensive move and took Rast to the floor. Shihan immediately got on top of him in what is called a Top Mount, or Tate Shiho in Japanese. They continued to grapple.

Just then, more students from both sides joined in and started fighting amongst each other. It was now Shihan and Sensei Rast, along with all the other students, fighting each other. It was a rumble. They continued to fight. Sensei Rast executed a reversal move on Shihan and took the top mount position, but Shihan countered with a guard sweep, knocking him off. Both men stood and circled each other.

The rest of the students fought with each other. It was forty versus forty. The fights continued with back-and-forth exchanges of martial arts skills. It was pure chaos.

Shihan and Sensei Rast continued to fight. Shihan said, "I knew you couldn't fight fair. You have never been a man of your word."

Sensei Rast replied, "I never told them to join in."

"You still haven't told them to stop."

The fighting continued for another five minutes. People on both sides were taking their licks and bruises, but in the end, Shihan and Sensei Rast were the only two still fighting, visibly exhausted. There was no quitting.

Sensei Rast came in with a side kick and sweep, taking Shihan to the ground. Just as he was about to deliver the winning blow, Shihan's wife's spirit looked down on him. She nodded, and Shihan smiled. Sensei Rast punched downward. Shihan grabbed the punching arm, flipped him over, got on top, and grabbed both lapels of Rast's uniform, applying a choke hold. As he tightened it, Sensei Rast began to go unconscious and then tapped the mat. The fight was over. All the remaining fighters immediately stopped. Sensei Rast yelled, "Yame." He wobbly stood up and bowed to Shihan. It was over, and Shihan's team won. The fighting was done. The world was safe again.

All warriors gathered together and left the arena. Shihan and his team had saved the Earth once again. Now they just had to hope that Sensei Rast and his students were honorable and would keep their word. For now, the planet was safe from evil. Washii and Fukuru flew overhead as they walked off. The battle was over.

Characters

Merrick

Weapon of choice is the Bo Staff, called Rokushaku Bo (Row Koo Sha Koo Bow).

His Tenshi Guide is the Eagle, Washii (Wa Shee).

Cody

Weapon of choice is the Manriki Gusari, the thousand power chain (Man Ree Kee Goo Saa Ree).

His Tenshi Guide is the Bear, Kuma (Koo Ma).

Teal

Weapon of choice is the Sword, Bo Staff, and Arrow.

His Tenshi Guide is the Wolf, Ookami (Ooo Kah Mee).

Kiara

Weapon of choice is the Kusari Gama, the Kama (sickle and chain).

Her Tenshi Guide is an actual Angel, her mother.

Hank

This is the boy who is a bully that Kiara befriends. His dad used to be a friend of Kiara's dad and ran a martial arts school. Hank always seemed to be a nice guy, but at one point he suddenly changed.

Sensei Rast

This is Hank's dad, who used to be friends with Shihan Allie. At one point, he closed his school and stopped teaching. He ran an underground fight group and started acting crazy.

Renshi Ryan

Shihan's top student and instructor at the dojo. Expert in weapons and grappling.

The Tengu

Long-nosed goblins. They are the main evil people.

The Kijo

A demoness, witch, ogress, she-devil.

Sennin

Hermit, wizard, fairy. The Master Wizard – Master MacGregor.

Kitsune – (Kit Soo Ney)

A fox with a long staff with a razor-sharp blade on the end called the Naginata.

Fukurou – (Foo Koo Row)

Owl.

Tora – (Tow Ra)

Tiger – Cheetah.

About the Author

Born in West Islip, New York, on February 1st, 1965, **Allie Alberigo** began his lifelong martial arts journey at just three and a half years old. The son of a Nassau County motorcycle police officer and a seamstress from war-torn Malta, Allie was enrolled in martial arts to build strength, confidence, and self-defense skills. What began as a way to channel his youthful energy quickly became a lifelong passion and purpose.

By the age of seven, Allie had earned his Junior Black Belt under the eclectic "Jerome Mackey" system, a style blending multiple martial arts disciplines. Encouraged by his cousin—a skilled martial artist in Aikido—Allie continued to train, eventually earning his Black Belt and developing the foundation for what would become a remarkable career spanning decades.

Outside the dojo, Allie's adventurous spirit led him to explore a wide array of pursuits—gymnastics, stunt work, motorcycle racing, horseback riding, archery, firearms, scuba diving, and even a vibrant career as a **rock musician**. As the frontman of several popular Long Island bands, including *Exciter* and *Pyra*, he performed alongside major acts such as Cinderella, White Lion, Skid Row, and Ace Frehley of KISS. His bands recorded albums and even appeared on local radio and cable networks multiple times.

Allie later transitioned into acting, training under **Michael DePasquale Jr.** at the Action Film Camp. His film credits include *The Cutoff*, *Watchusdie.com*, *Black Cougar*, *Tumbling After*, *Dishonorable Vendetta*, and The Operative as well as appearances on *Guiding Light*, *Sex and the City*, and *Black Cougar TV*. He also produced his own television pilot, *Dreamweaver*, and was featured on HBO's *Kickboxing Special* with Tokey Hill.

Today, Allie is a respected **eighth-degree black belt**, international seminar instructor, and keynote speaker. He has presented at the **Martial**

Arts Super Show (seven of nine years), served as **Head Consultant for Member Solutions, Inc.**, and spoken across the U.S., Australia, and the U.K. for organizations like MASOU and NEST Management.

As a lifelong educator, Allie is the founder of **Taking It to the Next Level**—a business coaching and consulting platform for martial arts school owners. He co-hosts the long-running podcast *School Owner Talk* with Duane Brummit, sharing decades of experience in martial arts, leadership, and entrepreneurship.

Allie founded the Long Island-based martial art school L.I. Ninjutsu Centers, which grew into a worldwide organization with 6 locations in Long Island and schools in Puerto Rico, Costa Rica, Bermuda, Florida, and Upstate N.Y. Allie has been the owner and Head Instructor of L.I. Ninjutsu Centers since 1991, still currently teaching classes in East Islip, NY.

A prolific author and content creator, Allie has written thousands of articles for *Martial Arts Professional, Action Martial Arts Magazine, Karate International, NAPMA*, and *Shinobi No Mono*. His published works include *The Beginner's Guide to Ninpo, 21st Century Ninjutsu: A Warrior's Mindset, Martial Arts Business 101: Hooyah—Living the Dream, The Five Gateways to Happiness, and his fantasy series The Three Kings books 1 & 2.*

Through his teaching, writing, and creative pursuits, Allie continues to inspire students and readers worldwide. His guiding philosophy is simple yet powerful:

"You should only have one goal in life — to achieve as many goals as you possibly can before you die."

www.ingramcontent.com/pod-product-compliance
Lightning Source LLC
Chambersburg PA
CBHW071204300726
48975CB00004B/1283